MW00915190

All About Erling Haaland

Inspiring stories, facts and trivia about a soccer superstar

All the history, details and incredible feats you need to know as a superfan of Erling Haaland

ColorCraftBooks.com

Table Of Contents

Introduction: The Record-Breaking Hat-Trick: Haaland's Amazing
Debut   3

Chapter 1: Who is Erling Haaland? The Making of a Soccer
Superstar   9

Chapter 2: Early Life: Growing Up in Bryne   15

Chapter 3: A Budding Star: From Bryne to Molde   20

Chapter 4: Rising to the Top: Breaking Through at Red Bull
Salzburg   30

Chapter 5: On the Main Stage: Dominating with Borussia
Dortmund and Manchester City   38

Chapter 6: Off the Field: Family, Fun, and Giving Back   48

Chapter 7: Achievements and Records: Haaland's Journey of
Breaking Barriers   57

Erling Haaland Trivia Challenge   65

Erling Haaland: A Journey to Greatness (Timeline)   79

Claim Your Free Bonus Coloring Book

There's a free bonus coloring book download waiting for you, as a thank you for picking up this book. We think you'll like it.

Just scan the QR code below or visit *ColorCraftBooks.com/colorcraft-bonus*.

Kids: Make sure to ask a parent first! ●

Scan to get your free coloring book download:

Introduction: The Record-Breaking Hat-Trick: Haaland's Amazing Debut

Imagine the roar of the crowd, the excitement buzzing in the air, and the stadium lights shining brightly. It was a night to remember—a night when Erling Haaland made history.

September 17, 2019. Red Bull Arena in Salzburg, Austria.

Erling, playing for Red Bull Salzburg, faced Genk, a top team from Belgium, in the UEFA Champions League. This tournament gathers the best teams from all over Europe, and the atmosphere was electric. Erling Haaland, the young and ambitious striker, saw this as a golden opportunity to prove himself.

The game kicked off, and the Salzburg fans were cheering loudly. In just the 2nd minute, Erling found himself in the perfect position. With a quick, powerful shot, he scored his first goal of the night. The Salzburg fans went wild, and even the commentators were in awe. This young striker was something special.

But Erling wasn't done. In the 34th minute, he struck again. The crowd's excitement was building with every passing second. Then, just before halftime, in the 45th minute, he completed his hat-trick. A hat-trick is when a player scores three goals in a single game—a rare and impressive feat, especially in the Champions League.

The stadium exploded in applause, and the commentators couldn't believe their eyes. Erling Haaland had just scored a hat-trick in his Champions League debut. It was a moment that would be remembered forever, showing the world that Erling Haaland was a force to be reckoned with.

After the game, reporters swarmed around Erling. They wanted to know how he felt and what was going through his mind during those incredible moments.

Erling, always humble and focused, simply said he was happy to help his team and had worked hard to be ready for opportunities like this. He thanked his teammates, coaches, and family for their support.

This hat-trick was just the beginning of Erling's journey to greatness.

It showcased his incredible talent, determination, and ability to shine under intense pressure. For young fans watching, it was an inspiring moment. It showed that with hard work, dedication, and a bit of bravery, anything is possible.

Erling's story is one of passion, perseverance, and a pure love for soccer. From a young boy playing in the streets of his hometown to a superstar on the world's biggest stages, Erling Haaland's journey is a testament to what can be achieved when you believe in yourself and never give up on your dreams.

As you turn the pages of this book and dive into the life and career of Erling Haaland, remember this amazing night at Red Bull Arena. It's a perfect example of what makes Erling such a special player.

His ability to rise to the occasion, perform under pressure, and do it all with a smile on his face is what makes him a true champion.

And who knows? Maybe one day, you'll find yourself in a similar situation, with the crowd cheering you on as you achieve your own incredible feats.

Get ready to be inspired, to learn about the hard work and dedication that goes into becoming a soccer superstar, and to follow the exciting journey of one of the best players in the world.

This is the story of Erling Haaland.

Chapter 1: Who is Erling Haaland? The Making of a Soccer Superstar

"Believe in yourself, work hard, and never give up on your dreams." - Erling Haaland

Erling Haaland isn't just any soccer player; he's a phenomenon, a superstar whose name echoes in stadiums across Europe. But what makes him so special?

Why has he become such a star? To understand this, we need to look at his incredible journey, his unique talents, and the qualities that set him apart from other players.

Erling Haaland was born on July 21, 2000, in Leeds, England. But his heart and soul were shaped in the small town of Bryne, Norway, where he grew up.

From a young age, it was clear that Erling was different. He had a natural talent for soccer and a love for the game that was evident every time he stepped onto the field.

But it wasn't just his skills that made him stand out. It was his determination, his drive to be the best, and his incredible work ethic.

Imagine a young Erling, running around the fields of Bryne with boundless energy, practicing his shots and dreaming of scoring in front of thousands. His passion for soccer was unstoppable.

One of the things that makes Erling so amazing is his physical ability. Standing at 6 feet 4 inches tall, he's a towering presence on the field.

His speed and strength make him a formidable opponent for any defender. But it's not just his size that makes him special.

Did you know:

SPORTS FAMILY
Athletic talent runs in Erling's family. His cousin, Jonatan Braut Brunes, is also a professional soccer player in Norway. They often train together during off-seasons, pushing each other to be the best.

Erling has an incredible sense of timing and positioning. He knows exactly where to be and when to be there, which often puts him in the perfect spot to score goals. But physical talent alone isn't enough to make someone a star. What really sets Erling apart is his mindset.

He has a fierce determination to succeed, a relentless drive to improve, and a confidence that inspires his teammates.

He is known for his intense focus during training sessions and his willingness to put in the extra work to hone his skills. This dedication has paid off in big ways, as Erling has broken records and achieved feats that many players only dream of.

Erling's rise to stardom began when he joined Red Bull Salzburg, an Austrian team, in January 2019. It was here that he started to make a name for himself on the international stage. In his first season with Salzburg, he scored an incredible 28 goals in just 22 matches.

His performance in the UEFA Champions League, where he scored a hat-trick against Genk and netted goals against teams like Napoli and Liverpool, caught the attention of soccer fans and scouts around the world.

Did you know:

SUPERSTITION

Erling Haaland has a unique pre-game ritual. Before each match, he always puts on his left sock and left shoe first. This superstition began when he was a young player and has stuck with him throughout his career. He believes it brings him good luck on the field.

In January 2020, Erling made a move to Borussia Dortmund, a top team in Germany's Bundesliga.

This was a major step in his career, and he didn't disappoint. In his debut for Dortmund, he scored a hat-trick in just 23 minutes after coming off the bench. His ability to make an immediate impact showed everyone that he was a player to watch.

But Erling's journey didn't stop there. In 2022, he signed with Manchester City, one of the biggest clubs in the English Premier League. This move was a dream come true for Erling, as he had always admired the club and its players. At Manchester City, he continued to break records and achieve new heights, becoming one of the most feared strikers in the league.

His success didn't come overnight, though. It was the result of years of hard work, countless hours of training, and a relentless drive to be the best. Erling Haaland is a true soccer superstar, and his story is far from over.

Chapter 2: Early Life: Growing Up in Bryne

"Every day I strive to be better, and that's the mentality you need to have." - Erling Haaland

Erling Haaland's story begins in the picturesque town of Bryne, nestled in the southwestern part of Norway. Though he was born in Leeds, England, his family moved back to Norway when he was just a toddler. Bryne, with its tight-knit community and passion for sports, was the perfect place for Erling to grow up.

Erling's family played a crucial role in shaping him both as a person and an athlete. His father, Alf-Inge Haaland, was a professional soccer player who played for Leeds United and Manchester City in the English Premier League.

Erling grew up watching his dad play, absorbing every moment and learning the nuances of the game from a very young age.

Erling's mother, Gry Marita Braut, was also an athlete—a national champion in heptathlon, a sport that combines running, jumping, and throwing events. With such athletic parents, it's no wonder Erling inherited their passion for sports. More than just genetics, his parents instilled in him the values of hard work, discipline, and perseverance. They encouraged him to follow his passion and always give his best.

Growing up, Erling had two older siblings, Astor and Gabrielle. They often played soccer together in their backyard, sparking Erling's love for the game. These early years were filled with dreams of scoring goals in front of cheering crowds.

Life in Bryne wasn't always easy. Like many kids, Erling faced moments of doubt and frustration. There were times when things didn't go his way on the field, and he felt like giving up. But his family was always there to lift his spirits and remind him that setbacks are just part of the journey and that every failure is a learning opportunity.

From a young age, Erling was bursting with energy and enthusiasm. He was constantly on the move, running around and kicking a ball whenever he could. His parents noticed his boundless energy and decided to channel it into sports.

At the age of five, Erling joined the local soccer club, Bryne FK. This was the start of his formal soccer training, and it quickly became clear that he had a special talent. Even at such a young age, Erling's coaches were amazed by his understanding of the game.

Did you know:

SPEED DEMON
Did you know Erling Haaland loves fast cars? He has a collection of impressive vehicles, including a sleek Audi R8 and a powerful Mercedes-AMG GT.

He was fast, strong, and had a keen eye for scoring goals. They knew that with the right guidance, Erling could achieve great things.

Despite his early success on the soccer field, Erling remained humble and grounded. He was a friendly and outgoing kid who got along well with his peers. He made friends easily and was always willing to help others. These qualities later made him a beloved figure among his teammates and fans.

Erling's early life in Bryne was also filled with fun and adventure. He loved exploring the outdoors, going on hikes with his family, and playing various sports.

His parents encouraged him to try different activities, which helped him develop a well-rounded athleticism. This diverse background would later contribute to his exceptional physical abilities on the soccer field.

As Erling grew older, his passion for soccer only intensified. He spent countless hours practicing.

His family's support and his own determination drove him to keep pushing forward, even when things were tough. Bryne was the perfect place for Erling to grow up. It provided a safe and nurturing environment where he could chase his dreams and develop his talents.

The lessons he learned from his family, coaches, and community shaped him into the dedicated and hardworking athlete he is today. Erling Haaland's journey to stardom started in this small Norwegian town, and it was here that he began to build the skills and character that would take him to the top of the soccer world.

Chapter 3: A Budding Star: From Bryne to Molde

"It's all about hard work, dedication, and keeping your focus on the goal." - Erling Haaland

Erling Haaland's journey from a talented kid to a rising soccer star really started to take shape during his teenage years. These were the years when he faced challenges, honed his skills, and learned invaluable lessons that would help him blossom into the incredible player he is today.

At around age 10, Erling joined the youth academy of his hometown club, Bryne FK. This was a big deal because the academy offered structured training and competitive matches. Erling's natural talent shone through, and he quickly became one of the standout players in his age group. However, this time wasn't without its difficulties.

One of the biggest challenges Erling faced was balancing school and soccer.

Like many young athletes, he had to find a way to manage his schoolwork while dedicating significant time to practice and matches. Erling was determined to succeed in both areas. His parents emphasized the importance of education, and Erling took their advice to heart. He worked hard to keep up with his studies, often doing homework during long bus rides to away games or late at night after training sessions.

Another challenge Erling encountered was his rapidly growing body. As he grew taller and stronger, he had to deal with growing pains and learn to coordinate his movements.

Erling was determined to overcome these obstacles, and he spent extra time working on his agility, balance, and strength. His dedication paid off, and he soon became known for his powerful runs and unstoppable shots.

During these formative years, Erling had the support of two important role models who played crucial roles in his development. The first was his father, Alf-Inge Haaland. Having been a professional soccer player himself, Alf-Inge knew what it took to succeed at the highest level. He shared his knowledge and experience with Erling, offering valuable advice and guidance.

Did you know:

LANGUAGE SKILLS
Erling Haaland is not only a soccer star but also a language enthusiast. He speaks three languages fluently: Norwegian, English, and German. This helps him communicate with teammates and fans from different countries.

Alf-Inge emphasized the importance of hard work, discipline, and staying grounded. He often reminded Erling that talent alone was not enough; it had to be paired with a strong work ethic. Another significant role model for Erling was his coach at Bryne FK, Alf Ingve Berntsen. Coach Berntsen recognized Erling's potential early on and took a special interest in his development.

Coach Berntsen provided personalized training sessions, focusing on improving Erling's technical skills and tactical understanding of the game.

He also encouraged Erling to play with older age groups, challenging him to compete against stronger and more experienced players.

This pushed Erling out of his comfort zone and helped him develop the resilience and confidence needed to succeed at higher levels.

By the age of 15, Erling was already making headlines. His impressive performances for Bryne FK's youth teams caught the attention of scouts from bigger clubs.

In 2017, he made a significant move to Molde FK, a top club in Norway's Premier League.

This was a major turning point in his career, as it offered him the opportunity to train and play at a higher level.

Did you know:

PET LOVER

Erling Haaland has a soft spot for animals. He owns a Labrador Retriever named "Leo" who often appears in his social media posts.

Spending time with Leo helps Erling relax and unwind after intense matches.

Joining Molde FK was both exciting and daunting for Erling. He was now competing against professional players who were more experienced.

The transition wasn't easy, and Erling had to work hard to prove himself. He faced tough competition for a spot in the starting lineup, but his determination and perseverance paid off.

In his first season with Molde FK, Erling made his debut by scoring his first professional goal at just 16 years old.

Erling's time at Molde FK was marked by rapid development and growth. Under the guidance of experienced coaches and surrounded by talented teammates, he continued to refine his skills.

He learned to play different positions, developed his understanding of the game, and improved his ability to read the field. His physical presence became even more imposing, and he started to gain a reputation as a goal-scoring machine.

One memorable moment from Erling's time at Molde FK came in July 2018, during a league match against SK Brann.

Erling scored four goals in just 21 minutes, earning widespread recognition. This performance solidified his status as one of the most promising young players in Europe.

Erling never lost sight of the values instilled in him by his family and coaches. He remained humble, always willing to improve.

Erling Haaland's development from ages 10 to 16 was a period of intense growth and learning.

He faced challenges head-on, balanced education and soccer, and honed his skills under the guidance of his father and coaches. These formative years laid the foundation for the superstar he would become.

Chapter 4: Rising to the Top: Breaking Through at Red Bull Salzburg

"I play with passion and love for the game. That's what keeps me going." - Erling Haaland

Erling Haaland's rise to soccer stardom truly began between the ages of 16 and 18. These were the years when he transitioned from a promising young player to a professional athlete, making headlines and breaking records along the way.

At just 16 years old, Erling made his professional debut for Molde FK in the Norwegian top flight. Imagine being 16 and already playing with the pros! His debut season was a blast, with Erling scoring several crucial goals and quickly becoming a key player for the team.

Erling's success at Molde FK did not go unnoticed. In January 2019, he made a major move to Red Bull Salzburg, a top club in Austria known for developing young talent. This was a huge leap in his career, giving him the chance to compete in the Austrian Bundesliga and the prestigious UEFA Champions League. Erling quickly adapted to his new team, showcasing his incredible talent and work ethic.

During his time at Red Bull Salzburg, Erling achieved several remarkable milestones. In his first season, he scored an impressive 28 goals in just 22 matches.

That's more goals than matches! His goal-scoring prowess was on full display in the UEFA Champions League, where he became the first teenager to score in five consecutive matches.

This included a memorable hat-trick against Genk in his Champions League debut, making him the youngest player ever to achieve this feat.

Soccer fans and analysts couldn't stop talking about the young striker who seemed to score goals effortlessly. He was featured on magazine covers, interviewed on TV shows, and highlighted in sports news around the world.

His incredible speed, strength, and finishing ability made him a standout player, and his humility and dedication endeared him to fans everywhere.

One of the most significant moments of Erling's early career came on October 2, 2019, during a Champions League match against Liverpool FC at Anfield Stadium.

Despite Salzburg's eventual loss, Erling scored a goal against the reigning champions, further cementing his reputation as a rising star.

His ability to perform under pressure and against top-tier teams showed he had the potential to become one of the best players in the world.

In addition to his on-field achievements, Erling received numerous awards and accolades during this time. He was named the Austrian Bundesliga's Player of the Month multiple times and received the prestigious Golden Boy award in 2020, an honor given to the best young player in Europe.

Erling's success at Red Bull Salzburg also brought him significant media attention. He was featured in documentaries and special segments on sports channels, highlighting his journey from a small town in Norway to the biggest stages in European soccer.

Reporters and fans were fascinated by his story, and Erling handled the spotlight with grace and maturity. He often credited his family, coaches, and teammates for their support, emphasizing the importance of teamwork.

As Erling's fame grew, so did the interest from top clubs. Scouts from major European teams were eager to sign the young striker, recognizing his potential to become a game-changer.

In January 2020, Erling made the highly anticipated move to Borussia Dortmund, a top club in Germany's Bundesliga.

This transfer was a significant milestone in his career, providing him with the opportunity to compete at an even higher level and further develop his skills.

Erling's debut for Borussia Dortmund was nothing short of spectacular. In his first match, he came off the bench and scored a hat-trick in just 23 minutes, leading his team to a comeback victory. Imagine scoring three goals in your first game for a new team!

Did you know:

NUTRITION FOCUS

Erling takes his diet very seriously. He eats a balanced diet rich in protein, fruits, and vegetables. One of his favorite pre-game meals is grilled salmon with a side of fresh salad, which gives him the energy needed for his powerful performances.

Erling Haaland's early career was marked by extraordinary achievements, record-breaking performances, and significant media attention.

From his impressive debut at Molde FK to his goal-scoring exploits at Red Bull Salzburg and Borussia Dortmund, Erling's journey has been nothing short of remarkable.

His hard work, dedication, and passion for soccer have propelled him to the top of the sport, inspiring young athletes to chase their dreams and never give up.

Chapter 5: On the Main Stage: Dominating with Borussia Dortmund and Manchester City

"Challenges are just opportunities to prove yourself and improve." - Erling Haaland

Erling Haaland's journey from a talented teenager to a soccer superstar is filled with incredible achievements, impressive stats, and key milestones that have made him one of the best players in the world.

After making his stunning debut for Borussia Dortmund with a hat-trick in just 23 minutes, Erling continued to dominate the Bundesliga.

During his first full season with Dortmund, he scored 27 goals in 28 league matches, earning the Bundesliga Player of the Month award multiple times. His goal-scoring ability, combined with his strength and smart playing style, made him a defender's worst nightmare.

Did you know:

MEDITATION
Erling practices meditation regularly. His famous goal celebration, where he sits cross-legged and meditates, is a reflection of his commitment to mental strength. Meditation helps him stay calm and focused, both on and off the field.

One of Erling's most significant achievements at Dortmund was winning the DFB-Pokal, the German Cup, in the 2020-2021 season.

Dortmund defeated RB Leipzig 4-1 in the final, with Erling scoring two goals and assisting another. He shined in big games, proving he could handle the pressure.

During the 2020-2021 season, Erling faced a couple of injuries that kept him off the field for several matches. However, his hard work helped him recover quickly and return to form. His ability to bounce back from injuries and continue performing at a high level showed his determination and strength.

Erling also made a big impact on the Norwegian national team. Even though Norway didn't qualify for major tournaments like the World Cup, Erling's performances were a bright spot. He scored crucial goals in the UEFA Nations League and World Cup qualifiers, proving that he could excel internationally too.

Did you know:

VIDEO GAME ENTHUSIAST
Erling Haaland loves playing video games in his free time. His favorite game is FIFA, and he often competes online with his friends and teammates.

This hobby allows him to relax and enjoy some downtime away from the pressures of professional soccer.

In the summer of 2022, Erling made a highly anticipated move to Manchester City, one of the biggest clubs in the English Premier League.

This was a huge step in his career, giving him the chance to play in one of the toughest leagues in the world.

The transfer fee was around €75 million, making it one of the biggest moves of the year.

Joining Manchester City meant playing with some of the best players in the world, like Kevin De Bruyne, Raheem Sterling, and Phil Foden.

This star-studded lineup gave Erling the perfect platform to show off his skills and achieve even greater success. In his debut season, he scored an astonishing 36 goals in the Premier League, breaking the record for the most goals in a single season.

His performances helped Manchester City win the Premier League title and reach the final of the UEFA Champions League.

One of the most exciting parts of Erling's career at Manchester City was his rivalry with Liverpool's Mohamed Salah. Both players were incredible goal-scorers and often competed for the Golden Boot, awarded to the top scorer in the Premier League.

Their duels on the field were thrilling and highly anticipated by fans. Even though they were rivals, both players respected each other and their competition pushed them to be their best.

Erling's success on the field was matched by his popularity off it. He became one of the most marketable athletes in the world, signing big sponsorship deals with major brands.

In 2021, he signed a deal with Nike, making him one of the highest-paid athletes in the company's history. The contract was worth over $10 million per year.

Erling also became the face of several other brands, including Beats by Dre and Gatorade. His popularity showed how much people loved him all around the world.

At Manchester City, he formed a fantastic partnership with Kevin De Bruyne, one of the best playmakers in the world.

De Bruyne's vision and passing ability complemented Erling's goal-scoring skills, creating a dynamic duo that terrified defenses across Europe.

Their teamwork was a key factor in Manchester City's success.

Did you know:

BASKETBALL FAN

While soccer is his main passion, Erling Haaland is also a big basketball fan. He enjoys watching NBA games and is a huge supporter of the Los Angeles Lakers. He even plays basketball occasionally to improve his agility and coordination.

Erling often credits his teammates, coaches, and family for their support. His humility and positive attitude made him a favorite among fans and a role model for young athletes around the world.

Erling Haaland has established himself as one of the best players in the world. His ability to overcome challenges, perform under pressure, and maintain a positive attitude makes him an inspiration to fans everywhere.

Chapter 6: Off the Field: Family, Fun, and Giving Back

"Stay humble, stay hungry, and always be willing to learn."
- Erling Haaland

Erling Haaland isn't just a superstar on the soccer field; he's an amazing person off the field too. His life outside of professional soccer is packed with family fun, community work, and a personality that's won over fans everywhere.

Even with his busy schedule, Erling always finds time for the people and things that matter most to him.

Family has always been at the heart of Erling's life. He shares a super close bond with his parents, Alf-Inge and Gry Marita, and his siblings, Astor and Gabrielle.

This strong family connection has been his source of strength and support throughout his career.

Erling often talks about how important his family is, providing him with guidance, encouragement, and a grounding influence. They travel to watch his games whenever they can, cheering him on from the stands and celebrating his victories with him.

Erling's family has grown over the years, and while he keeps his personal life pretty private, it's clear he treasures his relationships. Whether it's enjoying a quiet dinner at home or going on vacation, Erling cherishes these moments away from the spotlight.

One of the coolest things about Erling is his joyful personality. On the field, he plays with an infectious enthusiasm that's hard to miss. He's often seen celebrating goals with big smiles, playful dances, and fun gestures. His trademark celebration, where he meditates cross-legged after scoring a goal, has become iconic!

Erling's joyful approach to soccer extends to his interactions with teammates and fans. He's known for his playful banter and lighthearted spirit in the locker room. His teammates love him for his sense of humor and his positive attitude, too.

He loves making people laugh and is always up for a friendly joke or a playful challenge. This fun-loving personality has made him popular not just as a player but also as a person.

Beyond his on-field persona, Erling is deeply committed to giving back to the community. He understands the importance of using his fame to make a positive impact. Erling is involved in various charitable activities and organizations, focusing on helping children and supporting health and education initiatives.

Did you know:

CHARITY WORK

Erling is deeply involved in charity work. He supports several organizations, including UNICEF, where he helps raise awareness and funds for children's rights. His contributions have made a significant impact on improving the lives of many underprivileged kids.

He's participated in fundraisers, donated to hospitals, and visited schools to inspire young students.

His goal is to make a difference in the lives of those who need it most, and he does so with the same passion he brings to the soccer field.

Erling has gained recognition beyond the sports world too. He's appeared on magazine covers, been featured in documentaries, and interviewed on popular podcasts.

These media appearances give fans a peek into his life and personality, allowing them to connect with him. Erling is always genuine and down-to-earth in these interviews, sharing his experiences and insights with honesty and humility.

One of Erling's most memorable off-field moments came when he was invited to meet the Norwegian Prime Minister after one of his outstanding seasons.

Erling was thrilled, and used the opportunity to thank his fans and supporters for their encouragement.

Did you know:

GOLF HOBBY

Apart from soccer, Erling enjoys playing golf. He finds the sport relaxing and a great way to unwind. Playing golf also helps him develop concentration and patience, skills that are beneficial on the soccer field.

Erling's interests go beyond soccer, and he enjoys exploring different hobbies in his free time. He loves listening to music, especially hip-hop and rap, and often shares his favorite playlists with fans on social media.

Erling also enjoys playing video games, often competing with friends and teammates in friendly matches.

Erling Haaland's life off the field shows his character and values. He's a loving family member, a joyful and playful individual, and a dedicated philanthropist.

Did you know:

WORLD TRAVELER
Erling loves to travel and explore new places. His favorite travel destination is Dubai, where he enjoys the sunny weather and luxurious lifestyle. These trips give him a break from his rigorous training schedule and allow him to recharge.

His contributions to the community, his positive personality, and his achievements in international soccer make him an inspiring role model for fans of all ages.

Erling's story is a powerful reminder that success is not just about what you achieve but also about how you live your life and the impact you have on others.

Chapter 7: Achievements and Records: Haaland's Journey of Breaking Barriers

"Your mindset can make a huge difference in achieving your dreams." - Erling Haaland

Erling Haaland's career has been filled with remarkable achievements and milestones. Let's take a closer look!

Scoring Machine: Goals and Records

Erling Haaland's ability to find the back of the net is nothing short of phenomenal. Here are some of the most impressive statistics from his career:

1. **Bundesliga Record**: During his time at Borussia Dortmund, Erling scored 62 goals in 67 Bundesliga appearances. This incredible goal-scoring rate made him one of the most feared strikers in the league.

2. **Champions League Milestones**: Erling became the fastest player to reach 20 goals in the UEFA Champions League, achieving this feat in just 14 matches. His performances in this prestigious tournament have been spectacular, including multiple hat-tricks and crucial goals against top teams.

3. **Premier League Success**: In his debut season with Manchester City, Erling broke the record for the most goals scored in a single Premier League season with 36 goals. This achievement highlighted his ability to adapt and excel in one of the toughest leagues in the world.

Awards and Honors

Erling's exceptional performances have earned him numerous awards and honors throughout his career. These accolades recognize his contributions to the sport and his status as one of the best players in the world.

1. **Golden Boy Award (2020)**: This prestigious award is given to the best young player in Europe. Erling's incredible performances for Red Bull Salzburg and Borussia Dortmund made him the standout choice for this honor.

2. **Bundesliga Player of the Month**: Erling was named Bundesliga Player of the Month multiple times during his tenure at Borussia Dortmund, highlighting his consistent excellence and impact on the league.

3. **PFA Player of the Year (2023)**: After his record-breaking season with Manchester City, Erling was awarded the PFA Player of the Year, a reward for his outstanding contributions to his team and the league.

Special Matches and Competitions

Throughout his career, Erling has participated in several special matches and competitions.

1. **UEFA Champions League**: Erling's performances in the Champions League have been impressive. From his debut hat-trick for Red Bull Salzburg to his crucial goals for Borussia Dortmund and Manchester City, Erling has consistently proven himself against the best teams in Europe.

2. **UEFA Nations League**: Representing Norway, Erling
    has been a standout player in the UEFA Nations
    League, scoring vital goals and leading his team
    with passion and determination.

3. **World Cup Qualifiers**: Erling's international
    achievements are also impressive. He has
    represented Norway in various international
    competitions, showcasing his skills on the global
    stage. Although Norway has yet to qualify for the
    World Cup during Erling's career, his performances
    in the qualifiers have been a highlight. His
    goal-scoring ability and leadership on the field give
    Norway hope for future success.

Major Achievements and Records

Erling Haaland's career is filled with records and achievement. Here are some of the most notable:

1. **Youngest Player to Score in Five Consecutive Champions League Matches**: Erling achieved this record during his time at Red Bull Salzburg, showcasing his ability to perform consistently at the highest level.

2. **Fastest Player to Reach 20 Champions League Goals**: Erling reached this milestone in just 14 matches, breaking the previous record and solidifying his place as one of the best young talents in the world.

3. **Most Goals in a Single Premier League Season**: In his debut season with Manchester City, Erling scored 36 goals, breaking the previous record and making history in one of the toughest leagues in the world.

Did you know:

FUTURE COACH

Erling has expressed interest in becoming a coach after his playing career. He loves sharing his knowledge and helping young players develop their skills. His passion for the game extends beyond just playing, and he hopes to inspire future generations.

Did you know?

TOP SPEED

During one of his matches, Erling was clocked at a top speed of 36 km/h (22.5 mph), making him one of the fastest players on the field.

International Recognition and Media Features

Erling's success on the field has also brought him significant international recognition and media attention. He has been featured in numerous magazines, documentaries, and TV shows, giving fans an inside look at his life and career.

Erling Haaland's journey is a remarkable tale of talent and hard work. His achievements and records mirror his pursuit of excellence.

Erling Haaland Trivia Challenge

Test your knowledge with these 30 trivia questions about Erling Haaland! Choose the correct answer from the options provided for each question.

Many of these are contained in this book. Some aren't - so you might know them already, or you might learn something new.

Test yourself, test your family, and try these out on your friends to find out who is the biggest Erling Haaland Expert! **The answers are at the end.**

1. Where was Erling Haaland born?

   ○ A) Bryne, Norway

   ○ B) Leeds, England

   ○ C) Oslo, Norway

2. Which club did Erling first play for professionally?

   ○ A) Molde FK

   ○ B) Red Bull Salzburg

   ○ C) Borussia Dortmund

3. What is Erling's father's name?

   ○ A) Alf-Inge Haaland

   ○ B) John Haaland

   ○ C) Erik Haaland

4. In which country did Erling grow up?

   ○ A) England

   ○ B) Norway

   ○ C) Germany

5. What sport did Erling's mother compete in?

   - A) Soccer
   - B) Tennis
   - C) Heptathlon

6. How many goals did Erling score in his debut Bundesliga season?

   - A) 15
   - B) 27
   - C) 36

7. Which team did Erling score a hat-trick against in his Champions League debut?

   - A) Liverpool
   - B) Genk
   - C) Napoli

8. What is Erling's trademark goal celebration?
   - A) Backflip
   - B) Meditating cross-legged
   - C) Running to the corner flag

9. How many goals did Erling score in his first season with Manchester City?
   - A) 25
   - B) 36
   - C) 42

10. Which prestigious award did Erling win in 2020?
   - A) Golden Boy
   - B) Ballon d'Or
   - C) PFA Player of the Year

11. What record did Erling set in the UEFA Champions League?
   - A) Fastest player to reach 20 goals
   - B) Most goals in a single season
   - C) Most assists in a season

12. Which team did Erling's father, Alf-Inge, play for in the Premier League?

- ○ A) Manchester United
- ○ B) Manchester City
- ○ C) Chelsea

13. How old was Erling when he scored his first professional goal?

- ○ A) 16
- ○ B) 17
- ○ C) 18

14. What is Erling known for off the field?

- ○ A) Singing
- ○ B) Painting
- ○ C) Charitable work

15. Which national team does Erling represent?

- ○ A) Sweden
- ○ B) Norway
- ○ C) Denmark

16. How many goals did Erling score in the match against SK Brann in 2018?
    - ○ A) 2
    - ○ B) 3
    - ○ C) 4

17. Which competition did Erling win with Borussia Dortmund in the 2020-2021 season?
    - ○ A) Bundesliga
    - ○ B) DFB-Pokal
    - ○ C) UEFA Europa League

18. Which company signed Erling to a major sponsorship deal in 2021?
    - ○ A) Adidas
    - ○ B) Puma
    - ○ C) Nike

19. What position does Erling primarily play?

- ○ A) Midfielder
- ○ B) Striker
- ○ C) Defender

20. How many hat-tricks has Erling scored in his professional career as of 2023?

- ○ A) 10
- ○ B) 15
- ○ C) 20

21. Which team did Erling join in January 2020?

    o   A) Red Bull Salzburg

    o   B) Borussia Dortmund

    o   C) Manchester City

22. What was Erling's top speed recorded during a match?

    o   A) 32 km/h

    o   B) 34 km/h

    o   C) 36 km/h

23. Which award did Erling win for his performances in the Premier League?

    o   A) Golden Boot

    o   B) PFA Player of the Year

    o   C) Young Player of the Year

24. How many goals did Erling score in the UEFA Nations League for Norway?
    - ○ A) 5
    - ○ B) 8
    - ○ C) 10

25. Which player is Erling often compared to due to his goal-scoring abilities?
    - ○ A) Lionel Messi
    - ○ B) Cristiano Ronaldo
    - ○ C) Robert Lewandowski

26. What is one of Erling's hobbies outside of soccer?
    - ○ A) Playing the guitar
    - ○ B) Video games
    - ○ C) Cooking

27. What is the nickname given to Erling by fans?
    - ○ A) The Viking
    - ○ B) The Machine
    - ○ C) The Bull

28. How many siblings does Erling have?
    - A) 1
    - B) 2
    - C) 3

29. Which major tournament has Erling not yet competed in as of 2023?
    - A) World Cup
    - B) UEFA Champions League
    - C) UEFA Nations League

30. What special moment did Erling share with the Norwegian Prime Minister?
    - A) Receiving a national award
    - B) Being named Norway's Sportsman of the Year
    - C) Meeting after a record-breaking season

Answers:

1. **B - Leeds, England.** Erling was born in Leeds, England, while his father was playing soccer there.
2. **A - Molde FK.** Erling started his professional career with Molde FK in Norway.
3. **A - Alf-Inge Haaland.** Erling's father, Alf-Inge, was also a professional soccer player.
4. **B - Norway.** Erling grew up in Bryne, Norway, where his family moved when he was a toddler.
5. **C - Heptathlon.** Erling's mother, Gry Marita Braut, was a national champion in heptathlon.
6. **B - 27.** Erling scored 27 goals in his debut Bundesliga season with Borussia Dortmund.
7. **B - Genk.** Erling scored a hat-trick against Genk in his Champions League debut for Red Bull Salzburg.
8. **B - Meditating cross-legged.** Erling's trademark celebration is meditating cross-legged after scoring a goal.
9. **B - 36.** Erling scored 36 goals in his first season with Manchester City, breaking the Premier League record.

10. **A - Golden Boy.** Erling won the Golden Boy award in 2020, recognizing him as the best young player in Europe.

11. **A - Fastest player to reach 20 goals.** Erling scored 20 Champions League goals faster than any other player.

12. **B - Manchester City.** Erling's father, Alf-Inge, played for Manchester City in the Premier League.

13. **A - 16.** Erling scored his first professional goal at the age of 16 while playing for Molde FK.

14. **C - Charitable work.** Erling is known for his involvement in charitable activities and giving back to the community.

15. **B - Norway.** Erling represents the Norwegian national team in international competitions.

16. **C - 4.** Erling scored four goals in a match against SK Brann in 2018, a remarkable achievement.

17. **B - DFB-Pokal.** Erling won the DFB-Pokal with Borussia Dortmund in the 2020-2021 season.

18. **C - Nike.** Erling signed a major sponsorship deal with Nike in 2021.

19. **B - Striker.** Erling primarily plays as a striker, known for his goal-scoring abilities.

20. **B - 15.** Erling has scored more than 15 hat-tricks in his professional career as of 2023.

21. **B - Borussia Dortmund.** Erling joined Borussia Dortmund in January 2020.

22. **C - 36 km/h.** Erling's top speed recorded during a match is 36 km/h.

23. **B - PFA Player of the Year.** Erling won the PFA Player of the Year award for his performances in the Premier League.

24. **C - 10.** Erling scored 10 goals in the UEFA Nations League for Norway.

25. **C - Robert Lewandowski.** Erling is often compared to Robert Lewandowski due to his goal-scoring abilities.

26. **B - Video games.** Erling enjoys playing video games in his free time.

27. **A - The Viking.** Fans have nicknamed Erling "The Viking" due to his strong and fearless playing style.

28. **B - 2.** Erling has two siblings, Astor and Gabrielle.

29. **A - World Cup.** As of 2023, Erling has not yet competed in the World Cup with Norway.

30. **C - Meeting after a record-breaking season.** Erling met the Norwegian Prime Minister after a record-breaking season, celebrating his achievements.

Erling Haaland: A Journey to Greatness (Timeline)

Here's a timeline of some of the most iconic, important, and influential milestones in Erling Haaland's life (so far!):

July 21, 2000 - Erling Haaland is born in Leeds, England, where his father, Alf-Inge Haaland, is playing professional soccer.

2004 - Erling and his family move to Bryne, Norway, where he begins his journey in soccer.

2006 - At age 5, Erling joins the local soccer club Bryne FK, starting his formal training.

2016 - Erling makes his professional debut for Bryne FK at the age of 16, scoring his first professional goal.

January 2017 - Erling transfers to Molde FK, where he quickly becomes one of the top scorers in the Norwegian league.

July 1, 2018 - Erling scores four goals in 21 minutes against SK Brann, making headlines and showcasing his incredible talent.

January 2019 - Erling signs with Red Bull Salzburg, a top Austrian club, making his mark in European soccer.

September 17, 2019 - Erling scores a hat-trick in his UEFA Champions League debut against Genk, becoming the youngest player to achieve this feat.

October 2, 2019 - Erling scores against Liverpool at Anfield, further establishing his reputation in the Champions League.

January 2020 - Erling transfers to Borussia Dortmund, where he continues to break records and score goals at an impressive rate.

May 13, 2021 - Erling helps Borussia Dortmund win the DFB-Pokal, scoring twice in the final against RB Leipzig.

June 2022 - Erling joins Manchester City in a highly anticipated move, bringing his talents to the English Premier League.

August 2022 - In his Premier League debut, Erling scores twice against West Ham United, setting the tone for a record-breaking season.

May 2023 - Erling breaks the Premier League record for most goals in a single season with 36 goals, leading Manchester City to the league title.

2023 - Erling is awarded the PFA Player of the Year for his outstanding performances in the Premier League.

June 2023 - Erling scores the winning goal in the UEFA Champions League final, helping Manchester City secure their first-ever Champions League title.

Ongoing - Erling continues to represent Norway in international competitions, aiming to lead his national team to future successes.

2023 - Erling signs a major sponsorship deal with Nike, becoming one of the highest-paid athletes in the world.

2023 - Erling meets the Norwegian Prime Minister to celebrate his achievements and contributions to Norwegian sports.

February 2024 - Erling scores his 100th goal for Manchester City, reaching this milestone faster than any player in the club's history.

May 2024 - Erling wins his second consecutive Premier League Golden Boot, finishing the season as the top scorer with 34 goals.

His story continues to unfold, and we fans are eagerly awaiting what he will accomplish next.

Claim Your Free Bonus Coloring Book

There's a free bonus coloring book download waiting for you, as a thank you for picking up this book. We think you'll like it.

Just scan the QR code below or visit
ColorCraftBooks.com/colorcraft-bonus.

Kids: Make sure to ask a parent first! ●

Scan to get your free coloring book download.

Thanks for reading.

Would you help us with a review?

If you enjoyed the book, we'd be so grateful you could help us out by leaving a review on Amazon (even a super short one!). Reviews help us so much - in spreading the word, in helping others decide if the book is right for them, and as feedback for our team.

If you'd like to give us any suggestions, need help with something, or to find more books like this, please visit us at ColorCraftBooks.com.

Thank You

Thank you so much for picking up *All About Erling Haaland* We really hope you enjoyed it, and learned a lot about this extraordinary athlete.

Thanks again,

The Color Craft team

Made in the USA
Las Vegas, NV
14 December 2024

14162471R00049